*"Some women fear the fire.
Some simply become it"*

WARRIOR WOMAN ENTREPRENEUR

By
Mirav Tarkka

Copyright © 2020 Mirav Tarkka

All rights reserved.

ISBN: 978-1-7356711-2-3

COPY RIGHTS

The entire content of the pages of ("Warrior Woman"), including texts and images, is the exclusive property of MIRAV TARKKA.

All rights reserved. Any reproduction, distribution, storage or other use is prohibited without the prior written consent by MIRAV TARKKA Copying, altering, distributing, publishing or using on other sites for commercial use is not allowed this content without specific authorization.

MIRAV TARKKA reserves the right to any legal action, in any location and of any nature, in case of violation.

Release of legal, physical or property liability MIRAV TARKKA is RELEASED, WAIVED, DISCHARGED, AND COVENANTED NOT TO BE SUED, any liability, claims, demands, actions and causes of action whatsoever arising out of or related to any loss, damage, or injury, including death, that may be sustained to a person or to any property while participating in physical activity, or while on or upon the premises where an event is being conducted. MIRAV TARKKA DOES NOT SUPPORT any illegal or criminal use of the principles, skills, techniques and knowledge given and encourages individuals to use the information REASONABLY with proportionate force matching the situation, circumstances, environment and local laws or rules of engagement. MIRAV TARKKA DOES NOT SUPPORT the participation of minors or individuals with criminal records and or anyone with a mental condition or radicalised beliefs.

Legal Notice:

While all attempts have been made to verify information provided in this publication, MIRAV TARKKA does not assume any responsibility for errors, omissions, or contrary interpretation of the subject matter herein. While MIRAV TARKKA publishes what is considered to be safe tips and suggestions, the entire contents of the WARRIOR WOMAN ENTREPRENEUR is made available on an as-is basis, with no warranties expressed or implied. As such, readers use any advice contained therein at their own risk. This publication is not intended for use as a source of legal, ethical or moral advice.

The purchaser or reader of this publication assumes responsibility for the use of these materials and information. The author assumes no responsibility or liability whatsoever on the behalf of any purchaser or reader of these materials.

WHAT PEOPLE SAY

"Her courses aren't just about the moves you might use if attacked in the street, they're about mental strength. When you do your push-ups and sit-ups and other military fitness exercises with her, you're likely to have water thrown at you, or the other participants pulling and pushing you: you learn to fight on, ignoring distraction and discomfort. It's what makes the courses ideal for anyone preparing for a major life challenge, whether it be a marathon, a mountain climb or even a change of career."

Jonathan Freeman, Tatler Magazine

"Mirav offers a great balance and combination between psychology, criminology, physiology and NLP. It's a fantastic, realistic, dynamic, take-no-prisoners training program. Not for the faint-hearted, but more women should definitely empower themselves through this type of training. Very refreshing to be trained by a kick-ass woman in the mostly male-dominated discipline."

Yolande Herbst, Criminologist, and Human Behaviour Analyst

"Great technical preparation that unites the mind, body and spirit: these are Mirav's skills. During the interview, she impressed us with her charisma, her strength and her vast experience and physical capabilities.

"Mirav's knowledge is like no other; no one else comes close to her in Italy. Her methods are simply unique and very up-to-date."

Pamela Villani, Corriere Salentino

"She is young, small and fast with a contagious smile and an unusual self-confidence."

YOU magazine

"One of my most beautiful moments was to have met and trained with an extraordinary woman . . . very professional from a technical and psychological point of view. Loads of knowledge. She showed me how a beautiful woman can preserve her femininity while being strong and courageous and face her fears."

Dany Kant

"When I met her, I was in a place in my life in which I felt very weak, very belittled. After two hours of training, laughing, shouting and even playing, I felt like a new person. She didn't 'discover' my inner strength, she reminded me I'd had it all the time and I just needed to 'pull the trigger'."

Alex F

"Training with Mirav is like falling in love – before you know it you are doing things you never thought you would do before, and feeling like you have never felt before."

Shani M

"As a woman, it is difficult to find someone to understand your emotional and physical state when you are attacked. It takes one to know one, and her no-bullshit attitude helps to make you feel you are in good hands."

Sandra C

TABLE OF CONTENTS

ACKNOWLEDGMENTS	x
SHORT INTRODUCTION ABOUT THIS COURSE	12
ABOUT ME	14
ABOUT YOU	16
THE PSYCHOLOGY OF VICTIM AND AGGRESSOR	18
THE BIG SECRET OF SELF-DEFENSE: "YOU DON'T THREATEN A WHORE WITH A DICK."	19
THE LAW OF ATTRACTION	20
TRAINING YOUR DRAGON	21
THE DOUBLE-EDGED SWORD	23
THE HARSH TRUTH	24
OUR GREATEST ADVANTAGE, AND WHY DO WE REFUSE FOLLOW IT	25
THE WORKING WOMAN (YOU!)	28
WHAT CAN YOU DO NOW TO PREVENT VIOLENCE AT YOUR WORKPLACE	29
THE M.I.S.T.R.E.S.S. METHOD	31
CONCLUSION	55

(TAKEN FROM "UNDEFEATABLE"- MY AUTOBIOGRAPHY)

"From this moment on, you are undefeatable. No matter what happens to you, no matter what you are told, no matter what is done to you... it doesn't affect you. Remember that".

I will never forget the look in his eyes when he told me that. It is as if he saw my soul, saw how shattered I was, a thousand pieces, he carefully put them together again, and wanted to protect me. He was the only one who wanted to protect me, not even I had the power left in me to do that any longer.

At the time, my marriage was breaking apart. I felt guilt, shame, anger and grief, all at once. My 2 months old daughter needed me desperately, my 14 months old toddler wanted me all the time, I had to prepare for moving to another country, and I had to go through surgery. All alone. And I almost broke. Breaking means you just stop caring. You feel defeated, you have no control anymore of what happens to you. Life will happen as it wishes, and you will stand by and watch. You have no energy, you are drained, you are lost. When I came to him, I was almost there. I couldn't stop crying, I couldn't understand "why is this all happening to me"... I wasn't the perfect wife, but I didn't deserve this... or did I ? if it is happening, then I did, no? Here comes the shame, the sef-blame, the sabotage. I am not worthy.... and that point is the most dangerous one in your life. It is then when you are a really easy prey to all kinds of predators.

I was smart enough to look for something to pick me up. After all, I had 2 daughters to take care of. And I found my healer. But... the healing only started from him. He made me believe I can – and should- have control of my life again. I have been through worse, and I can go through this.

I wiped of my tears, took a deep breath, looked in the mirror and told myself I can do it. And I have been doing it every single day. What helped me alot is to set an ***empowering routine*** to keep day after day no matter what. I went to the gym every day at the same time, I sang and danced and played with my girls, I meditated, I trained my mind and I faked it- till I made it. Slowly but surely my power returned, I felt again in control of my life, knowing that I can- and will- do anything, survive anything, it is all in my mind.

In Israel, when life gets difficult, we say "Shayetet" (תשייט). It is the name of one of the Elite combat troups of our military, hardcore soldiers who can survive the worse conditions.

That was my power word. I would hug my children, tears running down my eyes, feeling the pain and the lonliness, and the fear of the unknown, and repeating to myself "Shayetet", I can do it.

The stronger I became, the better my life was. I won't lie to you, this past year has been very challenging. But I insisted. Things got better as I got stronger, and a year later, still alone with 2 toddlers, I know with 100% certainty I can do everything alone. I am an independant, smart, strong and powerful woman, no one broke me, and no one ever will.

Why am I telling you all this?

Well, I believe that, since you are reading this, you are or maybe have been in a place in your life where you feel weak, tired, empty, defeated. You are looking for ways to make yourself strong again, as fast as possible. I want to be your healer, I want to help you bring the best of yourself out. I want to look into your eyes (even through this pages) and tell you: from this moment and on, you are undefeatble!

And I will use my methods. I will teach you how to avoid probems and dangers, how to step away, how to use your power and body to defend yourself and your loved ones if needed, how to become stronger physically and mentally. When I asked "do you feel inferior to a man, physically" in my researches, most women answered YES. That they would never be able to defeat a man physically or even defend themselves enough to survive. No matter how strong you believe you are, this way to think makes you weak, and the lack of knowledge takes away a huge part of your independance. You are actually telling the world: I can't do it myself, in all times. I need a hero. I need to vry for help.

No you dont. You can do it yourself. And I will teach you how.

I found my streghth again, and I found it alot through my work and mission of empowering women all over the world to take control of their lives and actions, and live a happy safe life no matter what. I hope that from here on you will find your healing, your inner power, your inner heroes, yourself... UNDEFEATABLE

ACKNOWLEDGMENTS

In this manual, I would like to thank all my instructors, my martial arts and self-defence teachers (even those who taught me wrongly but also made me understand what I should really be doing), and above all my Krav Maga teacher Vincenzo Gaudino (Naples), who has patiently trained me for years, fine-tuning my military training, provoking my thought processes, and opening my eyes to the true power of mental training. A person I look up to as a teacher, but above all as a friend.

My professional staff, who took a huge loads off my shoulders and helped produce this course:

> My amazing editor Heidi De Love
> Parul Agrawal, our best-seller launching expert
> Deepak Gupta for the formatting of the book
> Diego Padron- my Shaman who guided me through some very challenging moments in my life, this book wouldn't have come to light without him.

Special thanks to my fans, followers, readers and all the women out there who have constantly been in my thoughts while writing and creating this course.

My biggest debt of gratitude can only be read and received years from now, and is to the youngest ladies in my life, my greatest teachers, my strongest motivation, my reason for everything: my little daughters Gaia & Xai. Whatever I do, I do for you. I will always do my best to teach you everything I know, protect you from all the dangers I can, and love you with my entire being.

With all my heart,

Mirav xx

A SHORT INTRODUCTION ABOUT THIS COURSE

WELCOME and CONGRATULATIONS for choosing this route to self-empowerment and strength. This course has been carefully tailored to suit your needs, necessities, limits of time and energy. Written for women by a woman, keeping in mind all the challenges we face as women but also our advantages. I know, and have "been there". My hope is that this guide will help you find a New You, a more Powerful You, an Invincible You. But before we begin some practical information.

ABOUT THIS COURSE

The manual will give you theoretical tools and information to help you achieve awareness, understanding and even some skills on the way to protect yourself.

This course will help you achieve:

- Immediate tools to help you RECOGNISE & AVOID violent situations.

- MENTAL training methods you can do at any time and in any place (without anyone noticing!)

- Increased self-confidence, independence and you will feel safer in your environment.

- The M.I.S.T.R.E.S.S method: 8 stages of self-defence, from the daily mental training to the physical confrontation, to create an easy-to-remember/apply system of self-defence principles.

- All of the above will allow you to work better and perform to your maximum capability, and create a different atmosphere around you, which will act as a defensive energetic shield against aggressors, reducing your chances of being attacked.

- For techniques, video course and advice you are welcome to contact me personally, at mirav@peppercoaching.online

IMPORTANT NOTE.

A word of caution: I will not go into the legal, moral and ethical aspects of your decision. It depends on local law, work ethics, your relationship with the aggressor and so on. I will teach you ways to eliminate the threat, and ways to just "delay" your aggressor (without hurting him severely), but the final decision is yours and I suggest doing your personal research into legal ramifications and inspecting your personal morals in various situations, because if you are ever attacked you won't have time to have that inner discussion with yourself.

ABOUT ME

introducing
Mirav Tarkka

I was born in Israel and lived there until I was twenty-six, serving in the Israeli Defence Forces for nineteen months as an operational sergeant and Krav Maga instructor. I studied psychology and criminology (B.A.) at Bar-Ilan University and physical education at Wingate Institute (both in Israel), departing for Italy after surviving several wars in and around my home town on the Lebanese border. It was in Italy that I opened my first training school.

I have been teaching self-defence all over the world for more than eighteen years, and have trained, fought, taught, been knocked out, knocked out others, been attacked, overcome physical and mental obstacles, learned several martial arts (my favourite was Muay Thai), travelled and researched. Personally, and professionally I have been through a lot.

Today I am a power coach, bestselling author of "UNDEFEATABLE", "ONE", "#STAYHOME" and "LADY X".

I teach out of experience as well as a wide-ranging knowledge, having gone through being attacked myself on numerous occasions even by those close to me, and having studied self-defence extensively. I have recently become a single mother of two girls. My children's safety, happiness and well-being, depend solely on me. This is how I fully understood the importance of my role as a mother and as a teacher. I practice what I preach, and I continue reading, learning and training, both mind and body.

My personal experience has taught me that the most important skill you can have is your ability to keep your cool, no matter what. Life will challenge you, test you and even mock you sometimes. Stay in control, don't panic and you will make better decisions, ensuring you remain as safe as possible.

And this is what I am hoping to teach you. I will show you tools that you can use to defend yourself against any aggressor, regardless how strong and nasty, but more importantly I want to teach you a new mindset (you will understand more about this further on). I believe with all my heart that every woman should enjoy control of her own life and have the knowledge and power to defend herself and her loved ones, preferably acquiring these skills before anything dangerous happens. This is what I wish to teach my daughters, and this is what I would like to teach you.

I see empowering women as my life's goal, and self-defence is one of my methods, as it covers physical, emotional and mental aspects and provides immediate tools to save lives.

This is a very important chapter in your journey towards self-love. You have to love yourself enough to want to defend yourself, as well as those close to you. We (women) are built for this. We were born to be protective (=maternal), possessive (=territorial), impulsive (=fast and great instincts) and sensitive (emotionally intelligent). No one can do this job better than you. And you know what? No one else should.

Prepare for the ride that can change your life and lead you to complete independence.

Now, let's get started!

ABOUT YOU

All women- as well as men- are born strong, protective and self-sufficient. It is enough to look at young children to see that; the lack of fear, the open mind, the will to "do it themselves", and the absolute knowledge that they are unique, and the world revolves around them ☺

The problem begins when we grow up. Insecurity creeps in, peer pressure, the media, our ego... we are told by others we are not good enough. We are not strong enough; we are not able to take care of ourselves. True, the world outside is dangerous. Violence exists, in many forms, always has and always will. But it is absolutely NOT TRUE that you can't have full control of your life and what happens to you- and I will prove it to you in this book. It is not true that you need help. You can do everything you set your mind to. Most people today look for the easy way out. Needing help and blaming others is the easier way out. Why assume responsibility? Why train hard, waste your time and energy reading, learning, training? Why even... think? Being like everyone else is much easier. Not questioning too much and believing what you hear gives you a sense of a "safe" life. But is it really? Who is safer, someone who relies on others to save them in case of emergency or someone who is able to save themselves when push comes to shove? How do we make the world a safer, better place for our children? By letting others control our lives or by taking the reigns ourselves?

You know the answer. You are reading this! You are one of the few that understands your personal power and responsibility. In Israel they say "there is not much space on top of the mountain" and this is what I want you to remember; you are unique. You are sufficient. You are powerful. No matter what "they" say. And "they" will always try to cut your wings, bring you down, tell you what you are doing is not good enough, it's a waste of time.... don't listen. Focus on creating the strongest version of you, inside out.

You are a potent, self-sufficient, resourceful and strong woman, always striving for self-improvement and empowerment. You love yourself enough to understand the need to protect yourself, and through experience you have understood that it is all up to you to learn how.

This course will create an even more powerful You. A woman who knows how to take control of her life and calls her own shots. A woman who is her own master.

It is likely that, at some point in your life, like me, you have felt completely powerless, helpless, out of control and out of focus. You might still feel that way on occasion. You might also feel angry that someone else has decided your future (or maybe continues to do so), your health, your body, your free time, even your smile. Your partner, your parents, a certain friend, your aggressor...

Well, that MUST change. No one should ever take away your power. You are one hundred percent entitled to decide what you do with your life, your body and your mind. You are responsible for your own choices. Now is the time to take this responsibility and honour it, make your choices with knowledge, with intelligence, and with the right mindset and attitude. Start to live a safer, fuller life, keeping aggression and violence far away from you. Having that mindset, being prepared for the worst, will put you in a situation where "the worst" will probably not happen. Murphy's law in reverse! Now you might be thinking, "Cool, I will do that, but some things don't depend on me, some things just happen. Bad things happen to good people, and I can still be chosen as a victim no matter what I do!" Can you still be chosen, or can you avoid it?

THE PSYCHOLOGY OF VICTIM AND AGGRESSOR

There is a particular symbiosis between an aggressor and his victim, a bond often neither side is aware of. They coexist, one cannot exist without the other (you can read more about this in the article I have written "Fatal Attraction" for CRGI magazine,

Part 1: https://conflictmanagermagazine.com/fatal-attraction-part-i-mirav-tarkka/

Part 2: https://conflictmanagermagazine.com/fatal-attraction-part-ii-mirav-tarkka/

Although I am not pointing an accusing finger at you (the "potential victim"), I am still giving you the responsibility for pre-training yourself in order to be able to handle different kinds of conflicts, and for the conscious and subconscious messages you leave out there to be read by others. This is actually a very positive thing for you, whether you have been attacked, are being abused or are taking this course to avoid that possibility in the future (smart!). But you have the power to never be chosen. You have already taken the first step. Learning and increasing your knowledge, understanding more, empowering yourself and your mindset is the true kind of strength and power that can never be taken away from you, and can only be sharpened and added to with time. Being strong and having self-defence training and skills is important and beneficial, but it is not the whole picture. You can actually prevent yourself from being attacked even without training by adopting the right mindset ("train your dragon") and that is what we will do during this express course. You will learn to think in a certain way, to see things differently, to transmit different vibes, and to keep reinforcing yourself. You will transmit a "don't-fuck-with-me" attitude, and you will be able to "read" people before they even notice you. You will know what to do in the worst-case scenario and you won't have to learn from experience . . . you can learn from the experiences of others and save yourself that trauma.

There are other things you can do to save yourself from being "chosen". Anything to do with self-love will work. The more you love yourself, the more you will transmit confidence. In very few words: do things that do you good, and make you feel good. Meditate, laugh, spend time with positive people, bring joy to your life . . . doing these is just as important as being aware of your surroundings and having situational awareness. When you change, your immediate environment will too. And when you are confident, strong and powerful, adding to this all the know-how in the pages ahead, makes it very likely you will never be attacked.

THE BIG SECRET OF SELF-DEFENSE: "YOU DON'T THREATEN A WHORE WITH A DICK."

In Israel there's a popular if somewhat crude saying, "You don't threaten a whore with a dick", the meaning of which is highly empowering: you should avoid provoking someone who might know how to fight back. An aggressor will look for a victim who is most likely weak, distracted or helpless. He will not look for a challenge. So, if you make yourself a challenge for him, it is unlikely you will be chosen! Just as a thief will look for a house with an open door, a broken window, or some other easy way in and out, rather than one with bars, alarms, cameras and a ferocious pit bull in the entrance.

Become that woman, the one attackers don't mess around with because there's no point: the fight will be too long and they might get caught or hurt. Transmit to the outside world that, no, you don't want to get your hands dirty and your manicure ruined, but if you have to, those well-polished nails will become as dangerous as the claws of a tigress. You were born to protect your cubs and yourself, and being a woman, being feminine, being a lady, doesn't contradict this. You will kill to survive. He will bleed from his own knife, be shot with his own gun, and beg for mercy before you are finished – because no one should mess with you, no one should force you to do things against your will. You know it, you feel it, and he will feel it. And stay far away.

THE LAW OF ATTRACTION

Like a magnet you attract events and people to you, whether negative or positive. Energy attracts energy of the same quality and vibration ("frequency") and, as known by the laws of physics and the law of attraction, your thoughts, your feelings, your moods and so on are all producing these vibrations that create an energy field around you (a "magnet"). Some days are bad and you draw bad events ("low" frequencies) while others are great and good things ("high" frequencies) just keep coming. It is unlikely that someone will pick a fight with you if you are walking firmly to work, happily "scanning" and looking around (using situational awareness- I will explain more about that later on), totally confident that if push comes to shove you can handle things. As the Latin tag has it, similes similibus gaudent or 'like seeks like', meaning not that an aggressor would look for another aggressor just like him, but rather that an aggressor will look for a victim who has the same frequency he has. All negative emotions have a low frequency and all positive ones have a high one, so if the aggressor is charged with anger, frustration, disappointment and so on, and the victim is influenced by stress, sadness, low confidence, fear and such, they will match. Like a jigsaw puzzle – if it fits the aggressor's, i.e. is submissive, he will be more attracted to you. If it doesn't match, he won't.

So how do you change your "energy field", your frequency, to "disengage" with your aggressor's? Simple. Since everything in life is energy (you, your thoughts and feelings, your friends and surroundings thoughts and feelings, the air, the plants, the animals, even your "still" environment) and energy vibrates and creates together an energy field, you just have to focus on "feeding" your energy with the higher frequencies. Thinking positive, communicating with positive people, making kind gestures, smiling, dancing, doing things that fill you with joy and pleasure, de-stressing and so on. The absolute best thing you can do (this is a bit more difficult and needs some time and practice) is to radiate an inner positivity which will be totally misaligned to any negative one, so strong that all "low" frequencies around you will be rejected or changed. That is the true magnetic power of your mind; changing your environment by your own power. The power that comes from within is the strongest and most effective. To achieve this you have to do some inner/spiritual work (meditation, reflection, etc.), a highly personal matter which lies beyond the scope of the present work, but I strongly believe that it is part of your journey, indeed anyone's, in this life of self-improvement, self-exploration and, of course, empowerment. Learning self-defence, however, will enhance and improve your energy field enormously and instantly. Have you ever noticed that when someone powerful or important enters a room, the whole energy field around them changes? Queen Elizabeth, the Dalai Lama, Oprah Winfrey, anyone who is considered powerful. Such people carry around a certain charisma, even euphoria, and this is what you will carry around yourself. Your training and knowledge from this course, and I hope you will keep on learning and training (especially your mind), will increase your confidence naturally and empower you. This will change the energy around you, from a "greyish" one to a "predatory" one. Your ongoing state of mind will contribute to this too. In addition, all videos and audios of miravselfdefense courses are silently charged with empowering and strengthening frequencies, that will reprogram your brain and do that extra work for you. You can and should keep this work going by yourself by listening to the right frequencies (just let them play around the house, in the car, etc.) and by active learning. As I said before, knowledge is true power and your power is always recognized in your energy field.

TRAINING YOUR DRAGON

Your mind is your best weapon. There are endless dangerous situations, problems and threats that could happen and can't even be imagined. Just as every person is different, so is every single aggressor, every set of circumstances – and every victim. So, learning self-defence techniques is excellent training (especially working on stress drills and reaction time), but it is not "the full Monty", the whole package. You might find yourself in a situation that no one has explained how to survive, or an aggressor you were never trained to deal with. But if you focus on training your mind and your mindset, you will arrive at a state of what I call Zen-like wisdom. True wisdom. Where not only you can sense, understand and avoid situations before they occur, but also your mind will quickly find solutions to address situations for which you weren't physically trained. Also, your body can fail you. You can freeze, get injured, be limited by your surroundings or your physical capacities. Maybe you are unfit, overweight or too heavy, maybe your sight is not so good or you have some physical incapacity. Your trained mind will always find solutions despite those limitations, and your trained body will follow your mind.

Let us consider, for example, the video course in which I explain about positioning. This is not a technique but a very important principle. Meaning that wherever you are, whoever you are facing, you have to try to get into a position where the aggressor has their back to you. Imagine you are caught unawares in a bathroom, with no improvised weapon, no one to hear you scream. It is small, dirty and slippery, and the guy is trying to rape you. You are so scared and shocked that you freeze, forgetting everything you have learned – but you recall the principle, because principles are easy to remember. So you change your position till he has his back to you, his front towards the sink or the wall perhaps. He can't see you clearly or reach you, whereas you can reach him, and with all your power, with no technical knowledge, you just push yourself explosively (another principle) against him. He hits his nose on the wall or head against the sink and you get the delay you need to get away. Mission accomplished. Do you need to be fit for that? Do you need to have perfect eyesight? Do you need to be a martial arts champion? Absolutely not. The only thing you have to aim to do is to remain calm and not panic (panic will lead to freezing), and in order to achieve that as a status-quo you have to constantly train your mind. Training your mind will also allow you to prevent certain situations long before they occur. You will learn to read body language and listen to your intuition, and most importantly trust yourself and your instincts (more about that in the "Basic Instinct" audio course you can download through the website). So, for example, when you are in your office, watch the door when it opens, know (and remember!) your clients and patients, figure out who might be dangerous, and always be prepared. If you have a new client coming in, you'll know him before he even opens his mouth; you'll quickly study his body language, his pace of walk, feel his energy ... and when you feel something is wrong, you'll reach for the alarm button or your phone, while grabbing something you can use as an improvised weapon. But it is far more likely that after one look at your confident, pretty face he will turn around to harass someone else or simply walk away. You are too much of a challenge!

THE DOUBLE-EDGED SWORD

Women are perceived as the "weaker" sex, emotional wrecks, a strong woman is usually seen as a bitch or butch, a sexual woman a slut, and so on. We used to be adored, worshipped! Women were goddesses, our sexual power was considered power, not weakness or sluttish but a choice, a respected one. When did all this begin? It started when men started feeling less masculine because their inner weakness prevailed over their outer strength. And what does a weak person do to a more powerful person? Try to take away their power. So year by year women were humiliated, enslaved, treated badly, tortured, denied their rights, hunted, killed, abused, raped, put down... and lost not only their power but their dignity and respect. Now it is time to change all that, to regain what was taken away and eliminate violence against women. I agree that there are huge physical and mental differences between the two sexes, but one being different from the other doesn't mean one is stronger than the other. We complete each other, men and women, and we are equally powerful. There is only one thing standing in our way: us. It seems that many women are far too comfortable with the submissive "Save me and take me to your leader" role. Of course, if so many women are OK with being used and abused so that they won't have to do anything by themselves . .

. our world will never change. As for my part, the one thing you MUST know how to do for yourself is PROTECT yourself and your loved ones. You can't just trust someone else will do this for you! Think about it for a second and realise, that in the worst situations of your life you were probably completely...alone! So turn your apparent weaknesses to your advantage! If you are short – you can quickly sneak under an aggressor's arm. If you are bulky – use your body weight as an explosive and amazingly strong weight and power. If you are exceptionally beautiful – use your looks to distract and dazzle your aggressor. If you have an annoying, loud voice (I am known to belong to this category!) – scream. If you are smart – manipulate your way out of confrontations. And so on! Multi-tasking, intuition, sensitivity, impulsive reactions … if men had those qualities the world would be… a disaster! We have to learn how to use all our qualities, and sharpen and improve them day by day as those qualities will be the ones to protect us.

We are our saviours.

THE HARSH TRUTH

That said, I want you to remember that YOU ARE A WOMAN. And although I will be giving you tools to survive, even with these skills and with a strong mindset you still are (most probably) not as strong as most men. Don't get me wrong; I believe that a woman can do whatever she sets her mind to do, and I believe that a woman can survive an aggressive attack and even reverse the roles. But, physically, a man is often stronger and bigger, and probably better trained. An aggressor will be "charged" to attack, by adrenalin and maybe also by chemicals (drugs and alcohol). He is ACTING and you will be REACTING. He knows his intentions and maybe planned them in advance, you will be taken by SURPRISE, and by the time you act, your reaction could be blurred by PAIN and FEAR. You have to think worst-case scenario; he is bigger, stronger, meaner, has hidden weapons and maybe other people to help him, it could be this is your really bad day, where your focus is clouded by fever, a fight with your boss, a quarrel with your partner, a sick child, a heavy heart. Maybe you are having your period, maybe you are sleep deprived. I will teach you techniques and ways to win the battle, but I am not going to delude you and sell you a myth that you can do it no matter what. There is never a 100% success rate, and there are situations, aggressors, and problems that we, in the "self-defence world" have no solution to. I know it's a harsh truth, but I would rather be honest with you than have you risk your life by living in a fantasy world. Knowing self-defence, practising it and most importantly adapting a different mindset will raise your chances of survival, teaching you how to avoid certain situations and sharpen your senses, your reactions, your intuition and also how to shorten your decision process. The untrained woman has a 30% chance of surviving an attack if she reacts quickly enough (less than five seconds). BUT a trained woman, and by "training" I don't mean physical training (although that will contribute to your power!) has already 50% or more in her favour.

*Note: these numbers have been taken from personal surveys among women who were attacked and women who were trained, as well as their instructors, police officers and centres for defending women from violence. Unfortunately, proper statistics and studies were not available due to the incorrect reporting rate.

Training regularly, physically and mentally, is very important, as REPETITION IS THE MOTHER OF ALL SKILL (T. Robbins). You can turn your mind into your strongest asset and you can turn your body into your protective shield by learning, training and repeating the same ideas, the same mindset, the same solutions. And I can teach you how.

OUR BIGGEST ADVANTAGE and WHY DO WE REFUSE TO FOLLOW IT?

The one thing that all women have that is stronger and better than men is our intuition. So why do we refuse to listen to it? When we were little, our intuitive thoughts were considered wild imagination and childish games. When we grew up, we might have been called paranoid, overly jealous and labelled with PMS or as "hormonal". I have one word to say to all that: BULLSHIT! We are women, we are human! Of course, we get emotional, angry and yes, even jealous. So do men! The fact that most of them are too scared to reveal their emotions and seem out of control doesn't mean they don't experience them equally. Yes, we have days when we are more sensitive and we cry more. On top of all that, we really need support and love and are probably not getting enough – which makes us even more sensitive... but not enough to call us paranoid! A personal example; When I was twenty weeks pregnant of my second child, one baby after another, I would cry at any Disney movie, get tired and stressed easily, I couldn't bear the thoughtlessness of people, for example, not letting me first in line although I was with a young baby and nine months pregnant. But that didn't mean I was in the slightest bit paranoid. On the contrary, my intuition was working ten times better. I was more tuned to sense dangers, potential problems and conflicts than I was ever before in my life. Listen to your intuition women, not to the men who tell you to ignore it! At the end of the day, YOU are the one who will pay the price for not trusting yourself. To distinguish paranoia from intuition, you have to practice listening intently to your body. It is like the difference between wanting to eat something and being truly hungry. Study yourself, get to know how your body works. Is your body signalling genuine fear or not? Until you can "feel" the difference, play it safe, so if you feel someone is stalking you, better to run and check behind you ten times than ignore the feeling just once and be . . . assaulted. So, what are the reasons which lead us to ignore what we feel?

- We let others convince us that what we feel is not true, especially if we have low self-esteem. Solution: work on your self-esteem, don't listen to other people.

- We are afraid to hurt others. Yes, many women don't hit back – not to mention hit first – because they don't want to hurt the other person. Sometimes in seminars when I talk about a rape situation (RAPE! Among the worst of crimes!) I suggest giving the aggressor a blow-job to ease him up, then biting his penis hard. Women look at me like I'm crazy, horrified and with disgusted expressions in their eyes. Or when I talk about plucking out eyeballs.

Seriously, do you love yourself so little that you would rather be raped than hurt your assailant???

- Fear of hurting ourselves. Yes, I agree, this is a problem. And I have to be honest with you – there is quite a big chance you will get hurt in some way. Maybe you can minimize the damage, maybe you can defuse the situation or escape before things get worse. But unless you are really able to avoid being chosen, avoid the confrontation and be well prepared... as a minimum you will absorb the first blow. So what can you do about it? Get used to the idea. Pain is inevitable. Suffering is optional (Diego Padron). In the moment, if you feel pain, accept it. Don't fight it. Observe it, feel it, acknowledge it, let it pass. It will. In the military we used to say that pain is a friend, as it signals you are still alive. In training, I would tell my students that pain is weakness leaving the body. If you can train pain, if you can get used to it, that's good. It will shift your pain/non comfort zone to the comfort zone. I am not talking about going and getting beaten up, but healthier ways like sports, training, finding the right competition, etc. It is part of your life, learn to control it instead of letting it control you.

- Not trusting ourselves My little 19-month-old girl would probably jump off the second-floor balcony – if I let her. She trusts herself that much. She trusts me that much. But we adult women have been told – convinced – that what we feel, what we think, what we want, is not true. We can't fight a battle. We can't go to war. We can't run for office. We can't leave our husbands if we are unhappy. We can't want more out of life. When I tell women, that they can win a street battle without applying force, just with their brains and mindsets, they look at me like I'm from another planet. "And if he's big", "What if he comes from behind?", "If he has a gun, then what?" and so on. The only thing standing between you and your aggressor is you. You are your worst foe or greatest friend. And it all starts from self-love. It is never too late to love yourself – and love yourself more. Self-protection is part of self-love.

THE WORKING WOMAN (YOU!)

Did you know that the majority of attacks happen to women at work or on their way to or from work? Women from all backgrounds are attacked each year in their work environment. Usually, by someone they know (a client, a patient, a co-worker, the boss, domestic violence that takes place at work and so on) and the majority of attacks are rape and sexual assault, robbery, aggravated assault and common assault.

The highest crime figures against women were reported for nurses, then professional care providers in mental health care institutes, then junior high school teachers and then store clerks. Among women, murder is the leading cause of death from a workplace injury.

(*Note: In this course we won't include attacks that might occur on the way to work (stalking, for example), at the parking lot, and so on; those are discussed in the second e book in this series, The Social Woman's Express Self-defence Course.

Whether you work as a nurse, a doctor, a psychologist, a policewoman, a lawyer, in a supermarket, in a bank, in a bar, as a model, as an actress, as a stewardess . . . anything that involves you being within physical "contact distance" (up to 7 meters) of another person, you MUST know how to defend yourself! And you must always be able to act in two different ways: you either hurt the attacker moderately, i.e. sufficiently to stop the attack and/or allow your escape, or you hurt him fatally causing death. The third option, which is for you to get severely injured or even killed, should not even cross your mind!

WHAT CAN YOU DO NOW TO PREVENT VIOLENCE AT YOUR WORKPLACE?

Here are a few basic things you can apply immediately, or ask for them to be applied at your workplace. Remember! A safe environment will create a better place for everyone to work and will benefit all colleagues. Everyone is entitled to this.

I. Talk to your supervisor (or, even better if you are the supervisor) to create a SAFETY POLICY, add some safety tools like panic alarms, visible cameras and warning signs, good lighting, security guards, etc. and frequently program specialised staff training.

II. Remember that it is your supervisor's duty to provide a safe environment for you to work in and violence should not be allowed in that environment. Workers need be able to complain and you should have details and access to that. If you hear or know about anyone in your work environment who is suffering from violence at work, urge them to complain and report it yourself, even anonymously.

III. Have an emergency service number available at all times, and if your workplace has no cell phone reception make sure you are able to reach a security officer in case of emergency. If that isn't available, get escorted to your car park, carry an improvised weapon at all times and get yourself well-armed, physically and mentally.

IV. Create your own "war zone" Here's the fun part! If you work in the reception area, position it in a way that clients or fellow employees can see you easily when passing by. At your office, position the furniture in a way for you to be closer to the door or exit, always facing the door (you have to see who comes in), always being able to exit easily without any risk of being cornered, don't put your desk in a room's corner. Prepare an improvised weapon within hand's reach, and toy around with it, learning how to grab it and use it easily. You can learn more about this in the video course.

 V. If you are handling cash -

  a. Keep cash register funds/float to a minimum.

  b. Favour electronic payment systems to reduce the amount of cash available.

  c. Change the daily times you count, empty or balance the funds, and always be aware of who's watching.

  d. If possible, change the cash's location and get a security firm, again if possible, to collect bigger amounts.

 VI. Have a "work sister/brother" as an emergency contact, to always know where you are or where are you going in case of emergency.

 VII. If you are travelling or meeting clients in public areas:

  a. When you go out for meetings or travelling, make sure at least one contact at work knows your location and contact details.

  b. If you are travelling for work, get to know the place you travel to as much as you can as fast as you can. Again, look for the nearest hospital and police station, have emergency numbers ready, know your routes and local environment and, of course, have an improvised weapon always within easy reach.

 VIII. Always check clients' credentials and details, play "detective". Knowledge is power.

 IX. Don't be a hero. If you have a hostage situation, for example, don't be the one to leap up and receive the gunshot so that others can go home. Your life is just as important as anyone else's. Life is not a movie and losing your life or getting badly injured is not worth it, unless you are protecting your close family. There are professionals like police officers, security guards, etc. specifically trained and chosen to be the heroes.

 X. The best defence is… avoidance! Avoid any situation in which you feel unsafe or uncomfortable! Don't go completely alone to meet a person you don't know, or without a backup, and don't put your job first at any price. Your life comes first! Always!!

XI. Be AWARE at all times of your environment, of who walks in, of improvised weapons, how things can be used against you and how you can use things against others. Know the names of people you work closely with (so you can call them for help, warn against danger, help them if injured and so on). Know the emergency exits, the staircases, the direction of the closest hospital and police station. Don't let your guard down; awareness can save your life and avoid tragedy! If anything feels or looks wrong or suspicious, listen to your inner voice. Refrain from going to the parking lot by yourself, avoid having your hands occupied, being distracted by your phone/ earphones/book etc. Avoid shadows, late hours, and so on. I can't emphasize enough how important this is! It will be discussed more later on in this e book.

XII. HARDEN YOURSELF as a target, and TAKE PERSONAL RESPONSIBILITY for your safety! You are, in the final analysis, responsible for your personal education and training. Read, train, think, not only to prepare yourself for a possible attack, but most of all to gain confidence and knowledge. Make learning self-defence fun, regard it as a new hobby, take a friend with you, make notes, do whatever works for you – but get your body and your mind sharp and strong so that if things ever turn bad, you can save the day. Your day!

THE M.I.S.T.R.E.S.S.™ METHOD

To make things easier for you, I have written down all pre, during and post stages of self-defence in eight points. To successfully defend yourself at all times, physical training is important, but most of all you have to adopt a different lifestyle and a different mindset, one in which you are aware of all your surroundings at all times, as if you are an omniscient god . . . or rather, a goddess! You know everything: who is behind you, who is in front of you, what's on the ground or around you, how far your punch can reach, how much battery you have on your phone, how much cash you have on you, who you can call for help, where the closest exit is, the fastest route to your home/police station/safe place, how long you can survive if you are bleeding, and so on. Nothing slips through the net. You are in total control, at all times. Even on your weakest days. The street, violence, the aggressor, will not accept any excuses, so always train your mind for the worst – and hope for the best. OK, let's make it super easy using an eight-point acrostic which spells out the vital word: MISTRESS!

1. MENTAL TRAINING

This is the most important and basic part of training, the easiest to do, but unfortunately the one considered the least by professional instructors. Among the many self-defence centres and training camps I have participated in, only in one have I been "mentally trained" (Naples), and I can tell you it has contributed to my mind far beyond my appreciation at the time. You see, your mind has to be able to switch in an automatic, robotic way from "peaceful" to "aggressive" in zero time. One moment you are sitting in your office, writing an email, having your lunch, filing your nails or whatever, the next your head is being smashed against the table, your nose is bleeding and you are in acute pain. Most aggressive attacks can be avoided in advance, and as I have written previously the correct mindset and energy field will prevent you from being chosen anyway. But we are not robots, we all have our bad days, and it takes time to change frequencies on a daily basis, as it takes time to build it up. You might be having a really foul day during which you broke up with your partner, your child had a nasty fall and your cat stands at death's door . . . so you are finding it hard to stay positive. I know, and of course, have been there! It is on a day like this that an attack might well occur. So training your mind to switch into "machine mode" or, as I like to call it, "animal mode" will allow you to react faster and save your life. In an average attack, the first five seconds are the most important. Five seconds! As a woman, your neck is so small and fragile, that even after a 3 second choke you could be already unconscious. You have to be able to not only react IN THE FIRST SECOND, but completely defuse the threatening situation within five seconds maximum. The longest time is the one needed for you to "understand" the situation and orient yourself. So, the training of your mind guarantees that your mind will switch in case of emergency from problem to solution in no time. You have to be as impulsive and reactive as you would be if you touched a hot stove by mistake, for example. You don't start thinking, "The stove is here, it is hot, I will pull my hand away." You just do! Same here. How do you train your mind to switch, to think faster and better? Training your mind to react fast is easier than you think. You can do it at any time, at all times, it will become second nature, and it will benefit you in many other aspects of your life, since – just as with your body – you will be able to think faster and act better also in everyday situations. The only "catch" is that, unlike gym training where you train for an hour or two and you are done, this is an ongoing task. You need to keep your brain cells constantly well-oiled, like an engine ready to run.

A few methods I have found effective:

1. **Play memory games.** There is no such thing as a bad memory or a good one. You remember something if your brain manages to dig up that part of the memory you want to use fast or gets lost in the process. The digging out part is what you want to work on. Why? First of all, any brain exercise increases your mental fitness – we call it "brain cardio". You want to work on the speed of your brain functions, to be able to act fast. Working on those memory receptors will work on your brain's ability to access information faster and faster, so in cases of emergency you can rapidly access a technique, a principle, an emergency number or whatever might help, but most importantly: you won't enter into panic (freeze) mode. In addition, being able to recall details afterwards, for example, a description of your aggressor, the area, the car's license number, and so on, can help identify the aggressor to the police and prevent further attacks if he got away.

How do you play memory games? If you have children, you could play cards, there are plenty of memory games on the market. But even in everyday life, try to remember simple, random things, and even play this with your friend or partner. In a restaurant, for example, try to remember (in a fraction of a second) the waiter's name tag, or exactly what they were wearing. When you're sitting on a bus or train try to get to know the names of nearby passengers and remember them, or those of clients (that is a great strategy, as it makes people feel more important, and creates a more personal relationship). If you are stuck in traffic try to remember the license numbers of cars in front of you, remember phone numbers, use your head to do sums instead of a calculator, and so on. Make it fun, give yourself plus points for success. Learn to walk in your own house with your eyes closed memorizing the number of steps you take, then place/misplace objects around you. Misplace/change objects in the fridge and the next day ask your partner to tell you what is different, try to learn and remember new words in a different language, among many other memory games.

2. **Interruption.** When you are doing something monotonous, washing dishes, folding laundry, filing your nails, etc. create sudden interruptions (for example; an alarm clock, loud music, someone patting you on your shoulder), and at that moment your reaction has to be fast and efficient. You could train in a gym with focus mitts – you have to turn when patted and hit the mitts – but also just auto-training can do the job. For example, you are doing the dishes and there is a church near you whose bell chimes every half hour, tell yourself not to watch the clock, but when the bell chimes, stop immediately and run to the door (for example) or lie down, as if the bell is a gunshot or an aggressor. This will keep your brain well-oiled and ready to switch from peaceful to switched on at times of stress. You can also program your alarm or music player, or try asking a friend to vary this kind of training. It is extremely effective.

Another amazing exercise: to train my "dragon" I would put on some very disturbing music – loud, angry, irritating – and in the background add my guided meditation or an audio course I wanted to listen to. Then I would try to banish the noise from my mind and concentrate on the words in the meditation/audio. The added audio should be played quite silently against the horrible loud music. This will train your mind to successfully concentrate on specific details and ignore the ambient noise. When you are attacked, the ambient soundscape you will have to ignore might be people shouting, traffic noise, alarms and so on as well as the voices of your inner fear/pain/panic, as well as your physical state: you might be tired, sick, injured or having your period. Your mind will switch to "tunnel vision" seeing only specific things, for example your aggressor's neck chain, unable to expand your vision or alternatively "360 vision", seeing everything around instead of focusing on what's in front. Everything might slow down dramatically as if you are watching a movie in slow motion, or else happen too fast. These are only some of the fascinating mind games your body will play with you as part of its defence mechanism. "Playing" with your brain in advance can help you deal with or even prevent these symptoms as you are bringing your mind to a known situation where it has to switch off some sounds/conditions and focus on what really matters. The important part is taking control of what you CHOOSE to take control of, and not letting the chaos around you control you instead.

3. **Scenario (imagination) games**. Make your life... a movie! Imagine scenes of attack and aggression and what you would do in that situation. For example, when you are sitting in a café (facing the door, of course), just think what you'd do, how you'd behave, where you'd go, and what you'd grab if someone walked in and started acting aggressively. Do not attach feelings of paranoia and fear to this, but treat these exercises as a game.

Regard them as if you were a director of a "good guys/bad guys" movie (in this case, good girls/bad guys!). This will shift your mind from potential problems to solutions, shortening your decision-making procedure in a real-life situation, and most importantly, the part of your brain that does the imagining, won't know the difference between reality and non-reality. Since in your "story" you have succeeded and survived an attack, the exercises of game-playing will slot effortlessly into real life and if anything, ever happens for real your brain will recognize it as a familiar situation where you have emerged the winner. Failure (= injury, for example) will be less of an option. Also, an unfamiliar situation is challenging for our mind and will require a certain adapting time-reaction in a real-life scenario. Bringing these situations to life in a non-reality version will create a familiarity within your brain that will shorten the reaction process – if need be – in a genuine emergency.

4. **Dialogues - "manipulating" people.** Another important strategy is absorbing as much information as you can about people around you or that you are in contact with, and giving out as little as possible about yourself. Knowledge is power, and in an aggressive situation, your aggressor is trying to gain power over you, in every possible way. The challenge you are facing is to allow him to feel as if he has obtained that power, but not, in fact, to give it to him. This is why I called it "manipulating". So for example, when asked questions by potential aggressors, people you don't know (you can tell your children to do so when asked questions by a stranger also) you can do one of the following things: -

- Answer with a similar question, in a non-provoking way or ask any question you can think of (avoid, though, asking him about his mother. It seems to provoke men!) e.g. (Aggressor) Q: "Are you from around here?" you could respond A: "You look familiar, are you from around here?" The aggressor will get worried you might know him or recognize him, in this case, and will probably look for an alternative, a "stranger". Also, questions engage the mind. Even if the question has nothing to do with the situation, for example asking all of a sudden what he had that day for lunch or what kind of shampoo he uses, will send his criminal mind elsewhere. His "program" to attack will be disturbed by the question, his mind will be seeking an answer, and you will either gain time, or his giving up on you as a prey all together.

- Repeat the last word of his question (you will either seem really stupid or he will start pouring his heart out!) e.g. (aggressor) Q: "Do you have a light?" you just repeat "Light?" It may seem weird but it works like magic! You can try it at home with your close ones or with complete strangers: repeating the last word makes people talk and talk – and talk. You will end up probably hearing you are a really good listener, when maybe you actually didn't listen to a word they said and just repeated the last one (long phone conversations with your mother-in-law for example).

- Lie. Fake name, fake address. Never upload details about your home address or when you are going on vacation on social media. It's like an open door for thieves, perverts, and stalkers! In the military service we had an exercise where we were instructed to go on a bus or train, and using these methods try to get as much information as possible about the person sitting next to us, without divulging anything about ourselves. That is an excellent exercise you can do! The main thing to remember is never to give out information about yourself, yet to avoid appearing uncouth in any way "Who are you to ask me that?" for example, is far too rude.

- An interesting technique from NLP (Neuro-linguistic

programming) is to try and gently imitate, or at least get close to, the sound of your aggressor's speech. Whether it is a certain dialect, slang, pace or volume, the more similar you are to him the more he will feel you are like him, and the less likely he will want to attack you. You are making him feel he is in his comfort zone, almost with his friends or peer group. This is a good technique also to use with clients, job interviews, and basically anytime you are looking to gain the confidence and trust of the person in front of you. You have to be careful, though, not to make it obvious or offensive. For example, a new client walks into your office and you want him to feel good and comfortable, even if he is not a potential aggressor. He is wearing a T-shirt that says JUVENTUS and speaks a bit louder and faster than how you usually speak. Say something like "I am a Juventus fan too! What a great team!" and speak a tad faster and louder than usual to make him feel instantly at home. Football fans can be complete strangers, even enemies, outside the stadium, but once there they all come together like one big happy family! He will probably buy what you are selling, and if he was actually planning an attack, he would probably look for a non-Juventus fan

5. **Reading body language.** To avoid problems before they even occur, you have to become a people watcher. It is a practice that quickly becomes second nature and it is also a very easy skill to acquire. Again, you want to be able to have more knowledge about the person in front of you than they know. There are many signs of body language that can indicate the person in front of you is looking for a fight or trouble, e.g., clenched fists, furrowed brow, narrowed eyes, shoulders hunched slightly forward, and possibly looking around nervously, hiding something in his hands and so on. It is important you exercise your body language skills on an everyday basis, see how people around

you place themselves when talking to each other when arguing, exchanging loving words, etc. You can easily start telling when a person is friendly or not, even if they have a fake smile. The first thing you should always look at is the person's hands. If you can't see the palms (hands behind the back, in pockets, in fists, crossed around his chest and so on), assume the worst; he is armed. Secondly, you look at the eyes. If he is smiling, for example, and the smile doesn't reach his eyes... something is off. Also, the pupils will dilate when adrenalin is released, so if he is already that close to you, you can actually tell when he is going to attack (but hit first!). Shoulders are also a good identifier of arm movements to come. By watching people, you will soon be able to tell by their shoulders alone what direction their arm is going to go to. Another great technique, again from NLP, is mirroring your aggressor's body language and stance. You don't want to be obvious and you don't want it to seem like you are mocking him. So for example, if he is standing with his hands crossed over his chest, and you are standing with your hands behind your body, that would create a sense of non-comfort. This is very subtle and it is subconscious, so you can "get to him" without getting to him physically! When you start watching people, you will notice that if they are having an intense, angry conversation their body language will be almost the opposite of each other's, whereas if they are lovers their body language will be almost the same. This works amazingly with everyone – clients, family members, strangers, friends. You can make them feel comfortable by mirroring them, or very uncomfortable by doing exactly the opposite. *Note: in job interviews or when there is a group of people or gangs, "mirror" the leader.

2. INITIAL PREPARATION

The famous "5 Ps", Proper Preparation Prevents Poor Performance, might save your life. Make it a habit before you leave your house in the morning to dress combat friendly. If at work you wear cigar skirts and high heels and you walk to your workplace or you have to go through a dark/possibly dangerous parking lot, put on something more comfortable to run/kick with and then change at work. I know, some women can do anything with heels, but the majority, including me, can't (not to mention the damage it does to your feet and spine), and as for the ridiculous idea of taking off your heels fast enough to use them as a weapon… that is close to impossible in the three seconds you have to react when attacked. Dress comfortably. Always have with you an improvised weapon. Metal keys, a rolled magazine, even a fork. I would avoid pepper spray as there are many factors there that might sabotage you (wind direction, spray might finish, and the spray sold to civilians is not that effective) plus the time you need to take out and activate is a bit too long, in my opinion. I would also avoid a pen or hairpin that might break in your hand. It is true that everything can be used as an improvised weapon, even sand. I had a student who was attacked and used dog poop to throw at her aggressor's eyes – and it did a good job! But since you are reading this, you can do better. My favourite to use is a Kubotan. Available online very cheaply, it is efficient, fits in your hand, creates a lot of damage, protects your hands from being damaged, and is completely legal in most countries. You can even pass through airport security with it. It looks like a key ring or sex toy. Remember! You are responsible to check the law in the place you live in. Not knowing the local law doesn't release you from responsibility or penalty! Practice with your improvised weapon frequently and in different situations and positions (both hands, closed eyes, lying down, running and so on) so you are quick and smooth in pulling it out and using it at all times. Part of your preparation is also having your phone charged, credit as well as battery. You can't make that life-saving emergency call if you're out of funds or have a dead battery! Also, you want to prepare emergency numbers on your phone ready to go. You need to have an emergency contact, e.g. close friend or partner, perhaps in the speed dial, which can be found easily on your phone by emergency services. Of course, have a prior conversation with that person so they know they are your chosen one (maybe even make a code word between you so they know when it is real emergency). Always have your phone, keys, and wallet on you, preferably front pockets. Have a note with emergency contacts written on it in your wallet and in your house, in case your phone is lost (most of us do not remember phone numbers by heart!). With regard to your wallet I suggest preparing two, a "fake" one you can present to the aggressor in a case of mugging, which might have expired credit cards, a few coins, etc.. Your "real" wallet would contain the important stuff, and you should keep it as close to you as possible (a handbag is not the best idea). Make copies of personal documents to keep somewhere safe in case yours are lost. Part of your initial preparation is also preparing your environment – your office, your car, your home. Always have a clear route to the exit, always face the exit, have an improvised weapon ready, and so on. Last but not least: take proper care of yourself. Although self-defence doesn't require physical strength, obviously the stronger, healthier, more flexible you are, the better. Avoid smoking, eat healthily, drink loads of water, sleep sufficiently, exercise, stretch, meditate daily and breath more deeply. Learn to keep a cool head and to control your emotions. Your body, mind, and soul will all thank you, and in case of emergency, your body will perform better and faster. Whatever age you are and condition you are in, do your best for yourself.

3. SITUATIONAL AWARENESS (SA)

You could probably avoid all potential aggressive attacks by exuding confidence, your body language, energy transmission and . . . situational awareness. Remember that knowledge, every kind of knowledge, is power. Knowing what is around you, knowing also your own body (see more in the video course about this) will put you at a great advantage, so great that you can transform prey (you) into predator (you again!). So whether you are walking outdoors, at work, in a public place, or even in your own home, always know what is around you, what can be used against you as a weapon, what you can use against others as weapons, the location of any exits, where there might be obstacles like stairs, a bench, an angry dog, a crowd of people, how far the police station is, etc. Always be focused. Avoid listening to your music with two earphones (you need to have one ear "tuned" to the outside), avoid being distracted (for example on the phone) and walk confidently even if you don't feel confident. People, like animals can sense fear, lack of confidence, submissiveness. But knowing all this puts you in a position to fake body language. Yes, it is better to be genuinely confident, but even faking it can buy you time, too. So, walk like you own the street, head up, back straight, tummy tucked in, stable pace, neither too fast nor too slow – don't drag your feet or look nervous – heel-to-toe step. All these are subconscious signs indicating your self-confidence, and an aggressor will be looking for an ill-confident, distracted person (again, you can read more about it in my article "Fatal Attraction") rather than a difficult target. If you have a bag, arrange it across your chest (not on one arm or shoulder), and always have something in your fist to use. The easiest, most available "weapon" to use at all times are your keys, so when you are walking (to your car, to your home) prepare them in your hand also to be able to get into a safe place (car/office/home) quickly but also to be used for self-defence. The best way to use keys is in a hammer fist (see my video "knock him out") with the sharp part of the key sticking out below the little finger, or between your forefinger and your thumb (also shown in that video) to create an extra impact when striking (temples, forehead, eyes, nose; anywhere in the face will cause bleeding and/or delay in the aggressor's reactions). You can also attach your Kubotan to your key set to add some interesting choices. If you are in a public place, always position yourself with your back covered (against a wall for example) and your face towards the exit. I was once sitting in a pizzeria in Tel Aviv, watching the exit and scanning around as usual, and a man walked in wearing a large coat. That seemed quite unusual to me as it was summer in Israel, so I left the table and went out, feeling something was off. And it was. A tremendous explosion followed a short time later, because the man was a terrorist and had explosives concealed beneath his coat. You see, you don't have to be a great detective or martial arts expert to save your own life. You just have to be aware of everything, and be prepared for the worst-case scenario. Scan around all the time. Look around, not straight ahead, all the time. Use windows, mirrors, car windows as ways to see what is behind and around you. Keep your ears attentive, your hands and legs ready for action, your mind alert. You need to feel, and see, if someone is coming from behind or to one side. You can't defend yourself from an attack you can't see. You need to be one step ahead of everyone, at all times possible. And, of course, avoid certain obvious dangers like dark or shadowed places when you are all alone, late hours, spooky places, and so on.

One word about screaming or shouting: don't rely on either of these as your exclusive defence tool. Most people don't run to help, they run away from trouble. There might be a situation where you can't be heard (loud music, hand over your mouth and so on). I am not saying to avoid screaming or shouting, but these are not the only solution by any means. Your mind and your body, are far better weapons. And if you shout, try something like "Let go of me, let go of the knife!" and so on. Because if you shout "Fire!" people might just avoid coming to help where they might get hurt. "Help!" is OK too, but again not that attractive to strangers, but shouting "Let go of me . . . let go of the knife!" will help you later in a court of justice, as you can claim self-defence, even if you injured the person badly. The "little old lady on the balcony" heard you telling him to let go of you or the knife, so there's proof you were scared for your life. Self-defence is also defending yourself legally, as far as possible.

4. TAKE ACTION (FIRST)

Now, you are already in a pre-confrontation phase. You can feel his breath, you can see his pupils dilated and his fists are clenched tight. Try to act as submissive and innocent as possible. He has to think he has already won the battle and assumed power and control over you. This will make the surprise effect bigger, and undermine his own defensive mechanisms. If, for example, he has a knife in his pocket, he might think that it won't be necessary to use this, as you've already surrendered. If you lift up your hands in surrender, keep your elbows close to your body, and your hands open with the palms towards the aggressor, in front of your eyes. So you are still defending your rib cage, neck and face. Look submissive, but be firm, meaning your hands shouldn't be weak and "mushy" if he pushes you. You should keep your balance and your hands are there to create a safe distance, a shield, between you and him (see video course "Stances"). Don't look into his eyes, don't look at his hands, look just underneath the chin (at the collar bone), bend your chin down so you look like a sweet little puppy dog, but you are actually limiting access to your neck. Tell him you don't want any problems, and that you are sorry for whatever he blames you for, meanwhile place your strongest foot a bit behind to enlarge the biophysical stance, and gesticulate with your hands (especially if you are Italian or Spanish!) so he gets a bit confused and used to them flying closer to his face ... "Please don't hurt me", "I will do whatever you want", "I would do the same if I was you" (that's a great one. Puts him in his comfort zone and it's true! But you will never be him), "We can talk about it if you want", etc. Try to make him feel at ease. DO NOT tell him to calm down. He will interpret the message as if you are telling him he is not calm, or you are ordering him around or acting superior to him. And then, whenever you can, in the minimum time and with the maximum power and explosiveness, HIT FIRST, HIT HARD, and HIT TO HURT. Attention here, ladies! I am not telling you to hit any harmless man thinking he might attack you. I trust you to be as intelligent as you are connected and attentive to your intuition. If you are in danger, it is better to hit first, if possible. Why? Because if you wait, in a second you will be hurt. Maybe severely. You will be in pain, in fear, and in great surprise. You might be bleeding, you might be being raped, you might be dying. DON'T WAIT! If push comes to shove, be the predator. Be the one to act, not the reactor. Feed him his own medicine, beat him up in his own game, show no mercy, and remember the whole time it is self-defence. Shout it, claim it, make sure everyone that can hear knows you are in danger and defending yourself. Even in the Talmud (part of the bible) it is written: "If someone comes to kill you, rise up and kill him first" ("להרגו השכם,להרג הקם"). The bible supports this idea, as it is about saving your life in a case of self-defence. "It is permitted to kill in self-defence, since the assailant forfeits his life and there is no guilt in killing him. We are therefore taught, "If one comes to kill you, rise up and kill him first". Even where the assailant does not directly threaten one's life, as with a burglar or armed robber, he may be killed in self-defence, where it may be assumed that he will kill if provoked" (Talmud). The Torah says "If a burglar is caught in the act of breaking in, and is struck and killed, it is not considered an act of murder" (Exodus 22:1). In other words, be that "early bird that catches the worm" in a way that doesn't let the situation escalate to one that you won't be able to react in (because you are severely injured, or worse).

David & Goliath (or, how to win the battle with any man)

As I mentioned before, a man is usually stronger than a woman, physically speaking. There are exceptions, of course, but to train your mind and body correctly, you have to prepare yourself for the worst-case scenario. So if he is a predator, a terminator, big, ugly and muscly, how do you beat him? The answer is simple. You don't aim for places where he has muscles but those where he hasn't. By producing the maximum damage in the minimum time, you eliminate one (at least) of the four factors mentioned below, creating either a delay or ending the attack. David did not beat Goliath by punching him. He aimed a stone bang at the middle of the giant's forehead, between his eyes, a point known to Chinese medicine as Yintang, or the Sixth Chakra, producing his unexpected downfall. (Remember: the greater the man, the greater the fall! You can turn his size to your advantage!) If you focus on power against power, your aggressor will always win. You can't fight against his weight, muscles or skills. You have to be smarter and go for particular points we call vital, focusing your blows on eliminating one or more of these four elements:

√ Breath √ Sight √ Mobility (joints) √ Consciousness (knock him out)

Only elimination of, or damage to, one (or more) of these four will create a delay in the reaction of an aggressor. If you practice self-defence or martial arts in a gym, remember to ask yourself this with every strike and move you practice. Many of the strikes taught do not serve you and will lead to possible scenarios that, in a case of emergency, will be difficult to tackle and might cause you permanent damage and even death. So you have to be very careful in choosing a self-defence instructor or school and, more importantly, you have to be an INDEPENDENT THINKER. Your aggressor won't always feel pain, so strikes to the groin area (read below) are not always useful. High kicks or "tornado" kicks are not fast enough in a dangerous situation, and they don't suit all aggressors or situations: you might lose your balance or be wearing something in which you can't kick high, he might easily grab your leg, and so on. A straight punch to the face (nose and mouth area) will probably do nothing but graze and irritate your aggressor. A man's face is quite a hard, bony area, and you are more likely to damage your knuckles (most women have a small fist) while inflicting little if any damage. A low kick to his thigh, used especially in Muay Thai, works amazingly well with men you might train with in the gym, causing them a "wooden leg" (immediate lack of energy at that place and pain), but it won't take care of the big nasty guy who trains MMA (Mixed Martial Arts), he is numb to that pain as that is a main goal in MMA and Muay Thai training, numbing the pain, and has decided to attack you. So, always focus on these four elements, and even if you don't remember everything, you're "supposed" to, just try to eliminate one of them.

The eyes are fantastic (even if he is wearing glasses) as not only do they have nothing by way of defence, but even just flicking water into them or making a gesture towards them causes disorientation and blinking. Taking away your aggressor's vision is one of the best things you can do, as he can't hit you properly if he can't see you. There are many ways to damage the eyes. The classic method from Krav Maga is to "pluck the eyeballs out" by pushing your thumb right into the eye socket. Now, I have seen this actually happen and it isn't as it's told. There are 6 (!) extremely strong muscles that connect the eyeball to its socket, plus nerves and fibres, built all in a spiral layout to protect the eyeball from inside. The force of these muscles around the eyeball is the same as the external anal sphincters and internal anal muscles! In order to pluck the eyeball out, you have to really shove your thumb in the angle of the eye and bring your thumb to the rear of the eyeball, severing the nerve and the main muscles. That would take you too long, and it isn't necessary. You can push with your thumbs into the middle of the eyeballs, yes, if you are close enough like in a rape position, or a close choke, or you can simply aim to scratch the eye with your nails (back of your hand) in an eye-flick or a "tiger claw" (see video about effective strikes). With both strikes you are safe from damaging yourself, and you create the delay you need. So it is not always necessary to "go Hollywood" in order to get the job done.

The temples are the soft spot in the face of every person, that actually have soft tissue and striking there can produce a knockout. You can do that with an elbow strike, a hammer fist, and any blow to that area.

The ears are also a great area to strike, as the aggressor will suddenly face a ringing buzz in them and will lose his orientation. Just turn your "normal" slap (I know you have one!) into an ear-slap, preferably a double ear-slap i.e. both sides at the same time. Cup your hand to create more damage (vacuum effect). You can also practically tear the ear from its place with just four kilos of force! The amount of blood the aggressor will lose plus the pain and mental stress will give you plenty of time to get away from the scene. You are probably feeling physically disgusted now, but may I remind you that this is both self-defence and self-preservation: it is your life at stake and you can't allow any space for mistakes, or even mercy.

The throat. Considering the fact that your aggressor will probably be a man, smashing, squeezing, flicking and pushing into his Adam's apple will create breathing difficulties at the very least. You can reach his throat with a punch, but better with a thumb (if he is close) or a "yoke" strike (hit with an open hand, making a form of a pistol with your index finger and thumb and using the fine space between them to strike. If he can't breathe properly, he won't be able to harm you effectively.

Large joints – especially kneecaps and ankles. It is a waste of time to go for fingers and toes, especially considering the fact that your aggressor will probably not feel any pain. Yes, it works beautifully in the gym, but how many of your gym members take pain-reducing drugs ;) ? The larger the joint, the greater the damage. But the easiest joint for you to damage is either the heel or ankle, just a simple shin or stomp kick, 360 degrees around the joint or the knee. These 2 joints are easily reached from every angle and will create lack/delay of mobility, which will work, of course, in your favour.

The groin area. Hitting a man in his groin will not create as much pain and damage as you might think. It is another myth of self-defence.

It will probably (though not always) create a reflex action of bending down and some kind of delay. You cannot rely on it. In the past, when aggressors were neither well trained and expecting a reaction nor taking hard-core drugs, etc., it was much more effective. But they have evolved, and so we have to, also. Moreover, you can't always reach the groin, and your strike will be quite transparent, obvious and expected. You might miss, and he might be wearing baggy pants, heavy jeans, even a groin guard. He might be standing with his legs close together, might be too tall, could move away, and yes, he might even get aroused by it (again, read my article! Very interesting.). So, it's OK to know this and to use it as a DISTRACTION leading to the next hit, so that he bends over as a reflex action to allow you to target his head which is now closer to you.

"DIM MAK" Karate points/pressure points, etc. There are pressure points in your body that can actually lead to death (Kill Bill style). Unfortunately (or perhaps not so!), only few can do this. You have to be trained and practised in these points to be able to strike correctly and precisely, or you risk targeting the wrong point, creating absolutely no damage or pain, and simply aggravating your aggressor. It is better to avoid a "Hollywood" move or something you are not sure of, which you perhaps saw in a movie, rather than risk your life. Stick to the basics and the principles. If you don't remember anything just remember this: go for the face or head. There you have the eyes, temples, ears and throat close by, and many blood vessels and nerves, so you will disturb, distract and slow down your aggressor for sure. After the face, go for the kneecap/ankle.

How to use your body as your weapon. I have explained about using an improvised weapon and your environment above, but there might be a situation when you have nothing to defend yourself with except your own body. The principles you should remember here are very important: when you attack, use your closest weapon to the closest target. Meaning, if your mouth is near his ear, bite it off, don't look for ways to necessarily get to his groin, for example. When you defend, remember that your goal is not to avoid damage completely, which might be impossible, but to minimize it. If it is a question of putting your hand in front of your neck when the guy in front of you is waving a knife, it is always better to lose a hand and not your life, or a finger rather than your whole hand, and so on. When possible to actually choose what parts of your body to use, the palm of your hand is better than the knuckles and the back of it, the heel of your foot is better than the toes, the shin is better to use than the knee. The smaller the joint, the more likely it is to break, and you don't want to spend time healing it. Try to use bigger, "safer" joints. If you are in a position to head-butt your aggressor from down to up, if he is taller than you, and you just go from underneath his chin with your head and hit him from the chin/jaw up, this is an amazing and very unexpected strike and you won't hurt your head very much. One last thing regarding your strikes; as you are probably lighter, smaller and less trained "in the street" than your aggressor, you have to use explosive power (see video "Be like a bee!"). You have to hit as hard as you can, in the shortest time, generating power from practically zero to 100% in the least time possible. Think of your strikes like a "bee", the aggressor should remain confused, disoriented, not knowing what hit him and not having time to defend himself. If you take your time and hit slowly, he will see what's coming, it won't be that effective, and it won't be that strong. In your mind, a second before you hit, take a deep breath, hold it in for a bit (this will help you also with the emotional control, see below) and..... bam! Strike! And don't leave your hand/foot/shin there- take it right back. Hit – and run!

5. REACT (hit second)

If you unfortunately reach this stage, you probably weren't paying enough attention to your environment and your instincts. You got hit first, so now you are suffering from pain, surprise, and fear. And you have to REACT. Your reaction will arrive after dealing mentally with the fear, surprise, and pain, and will be slowed down by factors like orientation, 360-degree vision, tunnel vision and other "mind games". The most important thing to do once you get hit is to get over these three factors; that is where mental training comes in very useful. Remind yourself that pain can be a positive indicator (meaning you're still alive), and whatever injury you're suffering from you will deal with later. Fear is your body's way to alert you that something is wrong, it is natural, accept it, embrace it, release it. You have to try to react immediately, as fast as you can. Your number one priority is self-defence. Liberate yourself from the choke, from the hold, from the grab, from the threat, in the fastest way you can. You can learn some techniques from the video clips. Your second priority is to block the next hit. Create space, and a shield, with anything around you – a bag, table, chair, car, etc. If you really have nothing to protect yourself with you use your body (bony parts like shins and forearms). Then, comes the attack. There is no defence without an attack, best to attack first, second best to attack while defending; one of the greatest secrets of Krav Maga!, and third best is to attack after your defence. Not attacking is not an option. You have to be as close to your aggressor as possible, in order to defend yourself from him and attack him. I know it sounds strange, but think of it this way: it is much more difficult to hit someone who is latched on to you, you have no range to punch or kick. The aggressor won't hit himself. You, however, have to know at all times, even if hurt, blinded, vision blurred or anything that keeps you disoriented, where your aggressor is. Grabbing at him or his clothes, will help you feel where he is, even in the dark. There is one exception though: if your aggressor has a weapon. I have not gone into weapon defines and retention in this course, so I will just mention one thing: if your aggressor has a weapon your goal is to keep the weapon away from your vital areas as much as possible, while keeping it blocked. You want the knife away from your neck, for example, and you will block the armed hand with your hands, and keep it blocked and away from your neck, as you don't want him waving around the knife trying to cut you. Show no mercy in your defence and attack. No rules, no limits, no mercy. He has attacked you first, you have now even less time than before, you have to create maximum damage because you have already been weakened. Use the principles explained in the last part, and practice some self-defence and attack techniques from the video course.

6. EMOTIONAL CONTROL

This is our Achilles heel, as women. This is the part we really have to work on, not to eradicate it from our minds, but to use it wisely in certain situations. Not being able to control our emotions in a stressful situation will lead to panic, freezing and an uncontrolled reaction that can also lead to our deaths. Cry later. Go to a therapist, break down in your own time. But right now, you have to keep cool and do the right thing for yourself. When you are in such a situation, remind yourself that whatever life has placed in your path, you can take control of the situation and reverse the roles. You are the boss, you are the goddess, you are the master (mistress) of your life. You are also an intelligent, strong woman. A very good and quick method to deal with any stressful situation, particularly an aggressive attack, to calm our minds and allow the body to act "panic-free" is breathing techniques. You can do this in seconds, and practice at any time. It works in a physical way as your brain is getting large and regular doses of oxygen. The most effective breathing technique for stressful situations is called "TACTICAL BREATHING" and was introduced by David Grossman, a Lieutenant Colonel in the elite U.S. Army Rangers. This kind of breathing helped firefighters run into burning buildings, police officers face armed resistance and soldiers fight in close combat. It is really easy to do, and I suggest doing it every day for three minutes, to get your brain used to it, and thus in a stressful situation to go into a familiar area of practised breathing mastered earlier on. What you do is "breath from your stomach", meaning balloon up your stomach when inhaling and empty it when exhaling, as if your stomach is your lungs. The counts of the breathing are important: √ Breathe in through your nose to the count of 4 √ Hold your breath to the count of 4 √ Breathe out through your lips to the count of 4 minimum (when you are more trained you can take longer) √ Hold your breath to the count of 4, this stage you can skip if you are short of time or feel uncomfortable √ Repeat until you feel your body and mind relax.

You might feel a bit dizzy in the beginning as your brain is receiving more oxygen due to the different and deep breathing. Don't worry: as your body gets used to it the dizziness will go away. See? Easy. Effective. Immediate. Very little training time and you'll prevent the biggest danger in an aggressive situation: panic.

7. SHISH KEBAB

Shish Kebab means minced meat cooked on the grill, which is what I call your aggressor once you've finished with him, the "grand finale" – and I'm talking about his mental as well as physical state. He must never ever even think of doing this again – to anyone. He must feel hurt, humiliated, embarrassed, and lost. He must learn his lesson. But, more than that, this part is to keep you safe as long as possible, till you reach a safe place. Here, you have to be heartless, free of religious scruples and vicious. There are no rules, no mercy. The man attacked you, and he is not your friend. He is your enemy. Don't wait until it comes down to "his life or yours": it's too late then. Choose yourself! You have tried to avoid, you have tried to defuse the situation, but nothing worked and he still attacked you. You managed to defend yourself and now it is time to finish with him and leave the scene. Do not depart without giving one last "security strike". You need to make sure he is as delayed as possible, because if you missed or if he faked his fall or pretended to be hurt, he may well have become even more aggressive. And even if you managed to strike him down, he might get up and go for you with all his might (don't forget he might be fuelled by drugs, alcohol, adrenalin, etc.). If he has a weapon and hasn't used it till now – this is when he will. So make sure his hands are empty, strike once more (don't stay for an hour beating him up), a good, strong, efficient blow, minimum time maximum damage – and run off. Go home, go to a safe place, and take yourself right away from the danger. The choice of how to finish is, as always, your choice. You need to be intelligent to secure yourself safe legally, of course as mentioned before, I will not go into that, but I just want to emphasize again one thing: when it comes to choosing YOUR LIFE or his death, the choice is clear. You do what you have to do. But don't "do first, think later", that is an irresponsible attitude. You think now, long before anything ever – if at all – happens. You think of possible situations, possible aggressors, and your solutions, your morality, your ethics, your legal rights, your red lines, and borders. Be as smart as an alley cat, and save yourself a lot of trouble.

8. SAVE OTHERS: REPORT & SUPPORT

This is the part where you are a hero, where you save other women and prevent the bad guy from doing bad things to good people. So many attacks and incidents go unreported. This not only creates the wrong statistics, but it makes women feel they are all alone in a world of victims/potential victims. We are not alone. We are a family. The family of women who were over time suppressed, humiliated, used and tortured. We want to take our power back. We are taking our power back, now, and we can't let these things keep on happening! This is your contribution to society, your duty to your fellow ladies, and your very important add-on to the empowerment of women. So please don't encourage the silence: there is nothing to be ashamed of. If something happened to you, report it in as much detail as possible. Go to the police, talk to support groups, shame the aggressor. If you have a suspicion that something is wrong with your friend, your colleague, your relative – try talking to her, make her feel she is not alone, that she doesn't have to deal with it alone. If necessary, report it. Talk to your supervisors to make your workplace safer. Create a forum, a Facebook group, a support group, to help women. We have the power to take back our power. Together we are stronger.

CONCLUSION

Congratulations!

You have learned so much in so little time, and you are now ready for the more physical part of the course.

Now before we go to the video course, I would like to return to some of the questions I asked you at the beginning of this e book:

How do you feel right now? _____

How strong do you feel from 1 to 10? _____

How safe do you feel from 1 to 10? _____

Do you feel less vulnerable when you are in the street, at work, in public? YES/NO

Do you feel more in control of your life? YES/NO

Do you feel you have achieved what you hoped for when purchasing this course? YES/NO

Your mindset started shifting. Again, not to a place of fear, but to a place of personal responsibility, of love for yourself and your loved ones. Things are different now for you. Your environment is different, your approach is different, and your confidence is rising, because you have taken this first step towards your empowerment, towards your training, towards your safety. Your next step will be a series of very simple video clips that will teach you important principles and a few useful techniques.

Training is important, but understanding the principles is fundamental. I hope you enjoyed and learned from this part.

Sincerely yours,

Mirav xx

P.S.

I know it is not easy living in today's world. It is still, in many ways, a world ruled by men, and women's rights and safety are not a priority in any way. I do believe that if we empower ourselves, become our own army, independently capable of looking after ourselves using all means necessary, and not allow others to take our power away, humiliate us, hurt us, emotionally or physically, things will change. I hope you believe this too.

Printed in Dunstable, United Kingdom